Atlas Sighs
Selected and New Poems

Alan Berecka

Atlas Sighs

Cover Image: *Sister Moon* by Steven Schroeder
Book Design: Rowan Kehn

ISBN: 979-8-9868994-2-8

Turning Plow Press

Table of Contents

Introduction

Writing about narrative poetry, the poet Louis Simpson claims, "Rather than to work himself up to a pitch of imagination, the poet would do well to discover what is there, in the subject. Let him immerse himself in the scene and wait for something to happen ... the right, true thing."* He continues: "There is a form of meditation that consists of keeping distractions away ... sounds from the street, itchings and ideas."

Alan Berecka's *Atlas Sighs: Selected and New Poems* offers readers a bountiful collection of narrative poems in which the poet, indeed, finds the "right, true thing" for each poem. A humorous presenter in person, Berecka's poems provide much more than comedy when carefully read on the page in the privacy of one's reading. We are treated to scenic displays of a poet who has immersed himself in memory, in focused scenes, created without distraction. His ability to create meditative insight, along with a vibrant, self-effacing, comical voice within his selected scenes from memory is remarkable.

In this collection, Berecka presents selections of four previous books, along with new work heretofore unpublished. A long favorite of mine is "Leveling," where the poet remembers "quietly" working on his mother's grave with his father. The scene is reconstructed in simple terms: "I wanted / him to think that I / had become a man." The poem wonderfully resolves with humorous insight: "Hey, kid, don't forget / how to do this." Other poems offer reflections on family occasions, his daughter's marriage, for instance, which is enriched by the frank admission of the unadorned reality of daily burdens, and wisdom from a long-married dad.

In *The Fall of the Leaf*, Berecka presents a more direct meditative style, and the meditation is rich. You will feel the depth of the poet's invention. Read these poems while imagining the subtlety of a cello reinforcing the themes – a complimentary, accompanying voice, to make a very satisfying experience.

His new work, like the preceding poems, provide insight and laughter on his familiar themes, which never feel tired: his Catholic upbringing and his continued search for the sacred in the mundane, the crucible of his extended family and heritage, his astute awareness of world issues, while maintaining an aesthetic distance that helps both poet and reader find a measure of reassurance. Perhaps the most powerful example of this last category is "Hearing of Uvalde while Visiting Vilnius." In this heart-wrenching portrayal, the poet cannot tell a weeping lady in the "basement / cells beneath the KGB museum" that he is from Texas. The poet concludes with stark honesty:

I cannot explain how it is possible
for me to walk or even stand today,
cannot explain why I am not wearing
sackcloth and ashes, how could I explain
that I come from a country that loves guns
more than life, a land where even our worst
tragedies just leave us numb.

Berecka's work begins with the literal – a place or a person in a place, and in his retelling, he takes the reader with him through the corridors of memory, reconstructing the psyche of both the poet and the audience. He accomplishes, almost naturally, what the poet and critic A.R. Ammons describes as "creat[ing] a vehicle, [that is] at once concrete and universal ... that is capable of bringing us the experience of a 'real' world that is also reconciled, a unified, real world." The poems in this collection "lead us to the unstructured sources of our beings, to the unknown, and return us to our rational, structured selves refreshed."

Ken Hada, author of *Come Before Winter*

* Simpson and Ammons are quoted from *Claims for Poetry*. Donald Hall, editor. Michigan UP, 1982.

from *The Comic Flaw*

An American Dreams

I stand waiting as Piusu Antonavage,
my great-grandfather, young, fresh
from the old country disembarks.
I find him on the pier, tired and gray,
smelling of cabbage and onions
being coerced toward customs
with little to declare.

With a large shepherd's crook,
I cut him from the flock
and plead with him to return
to where he belongs, where he
has always belonged. I tell him
no matter what he wants, he will father
an eloigned race. I plead with him
not to make this mistake.

His blue eyes, deep set, bleed
with rage. "You whiney bastard,
belong to what? There I have nothing
but starving mouths I cannot feed."

The cane now raised in his hands
becomes a giant red serpent.
Growing, its coils anchor my feet.

Weeks pass. He comes to me again.
This time I walk with my grandmother,
both of us children. We carry a bucket of beer
and change back from the corner joint. He sits
on a bright white porch where children play
at captaining ships. He pours a glass, drinks
deeply and grins. In a thinning accent he tells me,
"Boy, it is not so good to think so much.
What is there to know? Each man has one life.
What does it matter where he breeds or drinks?"

My Week as an Illegal Alien

para mis hermanos y hermanas

When I was a kid, Great Uncle Billy
let slip the family secret—his father,
Piusus Antonavage, was a fugitive.
Unable to get into America
through Ellis Island, the bullheaded Litvok
went north and then snuck in from Canada
crawling along the underside of a railway
trestle that spanned the St. Lawrence.

When I learned of my illegal roots,
I feared the worst and the INS
who upon finding out, would no doubt
deport us, the descendants of an ancient
crime, back to the Lithuanian SSR, back
behind the iron curtain where gray people
never smiled, never prayed, never played
baseball, and only ate borscht and boiled cabbage.

The fear festered for days until my mom,
who constantly studied the barometer
of her moody son's disposition, asked
me what had caused my current low to form.

Confronted, I confessed that I did not want
to be sent back to the old country and its older
ways. My mother, who spoke no English
until she was old enough to go to school,
the daughter of two legal Polish immigrants,
laughed. She said, "Let me get this straight.
You're worried because no one checked
your great-grandfather's papers?" I nodded.
"Son, relax. No one checked the Pilgrims' either."

Temperance

Each year come Ash Wednesday
my father swore off the sauce—
cold turkey for forty days
and forty nights of self-willed
sobriety. Our family's life
slid slowly off its hard edge.

Each night my parents watched
over my bedside Lenten prayers.
Finished, I'd climb into bed
and fall asleep counting
down the days until Jesus
would rise from the tomb
and the bottle would descend
from the unlocked cupboard again.

God's Radio

In Religious Ed a nun once told us that we
should always make the sign of the cross
before and after we prayed. The first gesture
opened God's wavelength, the second closed it off.

I wonder if the sister knew how many nights
I would lie in bed, panicked, wide awake
unable to remember if I had signaled
Roger and out. Odds or evens—heaven
or hell. I crossed myself without stopping,
hoping to land on evens or at least to interrupt
the feed before my memories of Linda Ceroni's
blouse and her fully developed fifth grade breasts
bubbled forth from the back of my pubescent mind.

Even as an adult, I find myself playing
the same game, while hoping that someday
I might cross myself one last time and be done
with it, but the deep need to hide always follows—
in the name of the Father, and of the Son...

Cleaned Ice

He always stopped the show, wide and big-boned
with a bald, bristled, many-chinned head.
He always chewed the same cigar's end
beneath his large red bulbous nose.
He never grinned, cared little for fashion
wearing black rubbers over his work boots.
He was past old. I knew that if he
belched it would smell of beer and pickled eggs.
Standing as he worked, he moved one hand.
He drove the Zamboni. I hated him.

From my nosebleed seat, I waited
for him to misjudge a corner, spin, bang
the boards, knocking the end screens out
of place. When he did, I'd clap and hoot,
"Hey, Jerkface, them's the brakes!" He
never looked up, but an old usher always did.
I slunk low in my chair, and prayed that Dad
would get back with my Coke and his beer.

Once the Eastern Hockey League could draw large
rowdy crowds, when the major league clubs
were too few, and the minors were for all the less
than greats and those older than great. Oh, they
were good, just not good enough to escape, so they
laced their skates for drunken construction workers,
zitted teenagers on the prowl, bored women
on soon-to-be-forgotten dates
and us—sons of all the above.

They were Armstrong, Anderson, Bannerman,
Hook, Babando, Kane, Kelly, Babiuk, Speck
and Smith—star members of the Clinton Comets
and small-town lore. I remember their goals,

their saves, their fights, and their blood
that stained the auditorium's ice, until

the Zamboni erased it all
with its slow and steady swipes.

Punxsutawney Phil Forecasts the End
of the Romantic Period

In an early spring north of the Mohawk,
or in the late winter anywhere else,
we fifth graders stood in line behind our teacher
waiting to be fitted and shod with rented
snow shoes for a short field trip onto what was left
of the melting snow and then past the pine-lined
playground, through the naked maples and birches
down to the thawing yet frozen Nine Mile Creek.

In an early fall east of the Trinity,
or in a late summer anywhere else,
we sat behind our thick anthologies
opened to an assigned page, slouching
in long neat rows before our professor,
who expected to guide us through the poetry
of the long dead Romantics and Victorians
and given time, the more newly deceased
Moderns, while we earned three credits
and occupied time and an air-conditioned space.

Just past the tree line halfway to the creek
some of us boys spotted it first, a woodchuck
that wouldn't move. We yelled to our teacher,
"Hey, over here!" Panicked, he yelled back,
"Don't!" He slogged through the watery snow
with the rest of the class to where we stood
enthralled. "Is it dead?" someone asked. "No,
just playing possum," some clown whispered.
As the nervous laughs died down, a timid suggestion
made its way through the pack. "Turn it over,
so we can get a better look." The teacher,
figuring why not, used the tip of his snow shoe
to flip the stiffened corpse. At first, its yellow
bucked teeth held my eye, until the girls screamed
and some boys grunted, "Cool."Then my eyes

were pulled down and found the pocket of maggots
swarming its exposed innards. Flustered, the teacher
suggested that we move on. Still, decomposition
remained the most impressive lesson we learned that day.

The professor read aloud each poem, and then once again,
stopping on certain words the second time through,
so he could point out the hand of genius that showed
through in the work's meaning and form. He lectured
on the nature of Aeolian harps and about the romantic romps
in which poets detected a benevolent yet unseen force.
I don't remember how it happened, but tiring of these dated
notions, something snapped. My hand, as if given life,
raised without my knowing, and then my voice was heard
for the only time that semester, and it was asking,
"For all the time that these guys spent in the woods,
didn't they ever stumble across a dead and half-rotten
woodchuck?" Our professor stared past me well out into space,
as if he was searching for the home planet of my alien
tongue. He then feigned an answer, shrugged and moved on.

Reconciliation

Any true act of forgiveness participates
in the sacrament of Reconciliation.
Fr. Efren Nano

As a child I spent my days playing
self-invented games with baseball cards.
I transformed my mother's well-kept den
into a not-to-scale replica of Yankee Stadium.
The *house that Berecka built* consisted
of reassigned furniture. The afghan
covered sleeper couch became the bleachers
in deep center. The footrest of my dad's recliner
became the screen behind home plate,
the assorted cigar and shoe boxes
that housed my collection were arranged
in a semi-circle and became the outfield wall.
Four Nestea baseball coins—three of plastic
for the bags and one of tin for the dish—
were laid out three feet apart on the green
shag carpet. A brown ceramic ashtray
turned upside-down became the mound.

I rolled empty Hershey's Kiss wrappers
into game balls. After nine cards
took the field, I hummed the anthem.
Play ball! I knelt beside the plate,
a hitter gripped in my right hand.
I flicked a pitch with my left thumb.
The batter swung. Some men dribbled
slow rollers that died in the high infield grass,
others ripped frozen ropes into the gaps.
Still others, like Mickey Mantle, possessed
the great power to lift the ball deep, pulling
Ballantine Blasts beyond the Thom McAn box
that stood down the line in shallow right.
As I dragged the Mick around the bases,
he limped his home run trot. As he rounded

third, he tipped his helmet to me. After crossing
the plate, he shook hands with his teammates,
who lined up to welcome him back to their dugout
that sat below the bottom shelf of our coffee table.

My mom never saw the stadium,
its invisible white facade, never thought
our television resembled the monuments
in centerfield. She only saw the mess and grew tired
of working on the grounds crew, straightening
the chewed-up field yet again. Like an ump
staring down an irate Ralph Houk, she warned me,
"Clean up this junk, or it will all get heaved out."

And most of it did get tossed that day
my best sluggers decided to relax
out on the field between the games
of a regularly scheduled twin bill.

At first my grief paled and confused her,
but she regrouped to say, "Some lessons
are harder than others. Besides, son,
you were warned, and what's done is done."

Still, I managed to keep a silent hope
that those cards had not been banned
but only suspended by a commissioner
whose punishments were known to be just.
Surely, she had thought this case through.
Once my lesson had been well learned, the Mick
and others would return from a secret place
to resume their careers. But as each birthday,
Christmas and Easter passed, I realized my cards,
like Gehrig and Ruth after their numbers
had been retired, were gone for good,

but not forgotten. When we were teens, my sister
bought me the "I'd be rich, but my mother threw out

my baseball cards" t-shirt, and I wore it everywhere.
One semester while in graduate school, I sold
my Roses and Carew's to pay for books.
I couldn't resist reporting back that my Mantles
could have covered my tuition and fees as well.

By the time my son was playing Pokémon
games with cards that I failed to understand,
the baseball card market had crashed,
and I realized that belting tin foil balls
for home runs with my cardboard heroes
had done little to preserve their value.

They were worth even less that night as I sat
my watch next to her bed at the cancer hospice.
Sedated she mostly slept, so the sudden sound
of her voice shook me, but not nearly as much
as her words which offered the grace to absolve us
both. "Son, I'm sorry...
                                    those damned baseball cards."

Leveling

Quietly, my father
and I worked,
leveling my mother's
fresh grave. We moved
in slow circles, raking
the broken earth flat.
We shook seeds
from handfuls of hay,
then covered the ground
with the straw that remained.

We didn't speak.
Nearly thirty years old,
I strained to stay
composed. I aped
his movements. I wanted
him to think that I
had become a man.

When we finished
filling and emptying
our watering cans,
my father, who cared
little for words, spoke
what I have come
to believe was his
greatest compliment:

"Hey, kid, don't forget
how to do this."

Coming to Terms

My father's constant commandment
focused on my hair, which he
had confused with some household pet.
"Train the damn thing. If you keep
it combed, it will learn to stay
in place." I listened to this heartfelt
yet blindly given advice again and again.

For close to two decades, I tried to keep
his law—"Keep thine hair combed,
so it may learn to fall to the right,"
but my hair had its own free will.
Its sense of order had been replaced
with one of wanderlust. Not even Daniel
could have tamed my wild mane,
nor could Moses, even with both arms
raised, have managed to keep it parted.

With oils, creams, and sprays,
my father anointed my head,
but my bad hair life went on,
until I was old enough to leave home.

Middle age brought me newfound
comfort with my hair, a chaotic mess
that hints at a more natural order of things.
It still falls where it may, but before I take it
on the three-day drive to my father's house,
it mainly falls on a barber shop floor.
Some say I have learned to use crew cuts
and ball caps to hide the truth,
but I prefer to see these simple acts
as humble sacrifices given in homage
to the most ancient of covenants.

My Life Among the Birds

My teenaged daughter raises three fingers
and turns her knuckles to me. She covers
her Texas twang with a fake New York accent
and tells me, "Hey, yuz da poet, Mister
Library-man, read between dees lines."

I took bird watching in college, science credits
for my English degree. The flunk-out course
for biology majors, I took it on a lark
from the great protector of the golden
cheek warbler—a man with no sense
of humor. For lab exams he asked us
to identify eyeless, avian corpses stuffed
with cotton. Stumped often, I would write
down *dead bird* and plead for partial credit.

When my sister and I were small, we learned
never to make the same request three times
to our father. "Can we go?" "Hell, no." "Please,
Dad?" "Go whistle." "Aw, come on!" "Kiss
me." He'd raise his extended middle finger
to his lips and blow us a mock kiss. As his
kids aged, we began to realize that flipping
the bird to one's children was less than normal,
so we'd invite our friends over and begin
to coax the birdman into his stale and profane
vaudevillian act to watch their shock and delight.

At the Aransas Refuge, the tower stands
forty feet high. Tourists flock up the concrete
ramps to reconnoiter the marsh, hoping
to catch sight of the whooping cranes.
Casual watchers often point out
graceful living semiquavers, bestowing
upon the common Great White Heron
celebrity status. The proud holder

of three credits in Avian Ecology,
I never correct them as they leave happy,
believing that their time has been well spent.

On this trip up north, I recall how my daughter
howled with laughter the first time she saw
my father flip me off. She now prides herself
on what she thinks is an artful imitation
of the old act. I have flown home by myself
to visit my recently stroke-stricken father. I sit
next to my sister waiting to learn the old man's
prognosis. The doctor enters and informs us
that the stroke has left him nearly blind
and has erased his vocabulary except for two words:
fuck and *no*. The doctor is taken aback
by our show of relief, so we explain that we
rarely, if ever, heard our father say anything else.

For My Daughter as She Leaves Home

In my boyhood, I learned two legends—myths
about the Eucharist. In both tales a priest
loses faith, one while he walked to visit
the sick while carrying a host pressed
in the pages of his breviary. The other fell
into despair and doubt as he raised the wafer,
as he stood behind the altar at the moment
of consecration. When each looked again,
they found instead of bread, slivers of meat
centered in small pools of blood. The legends
state that scientists came to test the flesh
and in both cases found it to be human,
most likely extracted from a heart. Faith
returned to the priests. The transformed hosts
survive as relics, the objects of adoration.

I do not know what to think of these tales.
I find it hard to accept the miraculous.
Still, once you have moved on from here,
should you lose faith in your own worth
or in the fact that you are loved, I pray
that this cheap piece of paper on which I
have labored with my simple art might
become a sliver of my own certain heart.

Meaning

It's only the second time in history we've had snow on Christmas...Larry Maifeld, National Weather Service, *Corpus Christi Caller-Times*, December 26, 2004

Christmas Eve Mass—
my kids serving,
my wife reading.
Barely Catholic,
I sit alone next
to the side exit,
on my mark, waiting
for the final blessing.

"Amen." I race.
First to the door,
a half-step out.
Snow. Snow
falling, dancing,
reflecting lights,
filling the night,
coating cars,
palm trees,
everything.

"It's snowing,"
I let slip.
The guy two steps
back laughs.
I hold the door,
then walk on.
He says,
"It's snowing."
The guy behind
him laughs...

One by one,
the church empties

out into belief.

I stand grinning.
Joined by my family,
giddy, we watch
as miracle
upon miracle
silently piles up.

Commuting

How far can a fog lift
before it becomes a cloud?

Whatever it was, it hung
above the causeway,
a few feet above each car
and truck, as we drove
over the shallow end
of the Gulf, consumed
with the needs
of our daily commute.

I noticed how the gulls
and pelicans disappeared
diving up into the thickness
but thought little of it, until
I rounded the long curve
near the final exit,
and there it hung
like a shroud, completely
obscuring the upper two-thirds
of the Harbor Bridge.

While being pulled along
by the constant traffic,
I watched the countless
sets of tail lights
ascending into obscurity,
taking on faith that beyond
it still lies the bridge
into the city of Corpus Christi.

from *Remembering the Body*

My Bone of Contention with Roethke

I knew a woman lovely in her bones.

I know a woman lovely,
and I mean lovely, in her flesh.
It hangs on her deep, like snow
on a January pine. In places she
seems more liquid than solid.
Think axle-deep mud, and, Lord,
how I love to sink in those ruts,
sending ripples of movement
in every direction, while I hang on,
riding the waves, and she with her knees
and toes pointing at the saints,
arms around me like she's crawling
through the air, carrying me
somewhere better than fine.

Theodore you can sing your praises
of your woman's fine bones, but
I'll be listening for the melody
of corduroy stretched tightly
across my love's thick thighs,
a lullaby that sets me to dreaming
about taking a dip in her singing flesh.
There will be time enough spent
with bones and dust, but until then
let me drown smothered
in my good mate's flesh.

McDemption

Against my doctor-ordered, low-fat,
low-sodium diet, I sat choking down
a Quarter Pounder Extra Value Meal,
as a bag lady returned her fries a second time.
She stuttered her anger at a zit-speckled kid
until a manager arrived to stand behind
the counter. The summoned man searched
for meaning in her barrage of spit and phonemes.
He apologized and explained that he wasn't sure
what she was getting at. Agitated even more,
she tried to reply but got stuck on the letter *b*
for so long that I thought she might break
into a doo-wop song. Finally, she said, *B-b-
browner.* I watched the man's face. I expected
him to say, "Look, lady this ain't the Ritz;
it's a freaking McDonald's!" But instead
he took the fries and said, "Let me see
what I can do." As he walked away, she grinned.
And maybe it was all the salt I had ingested,
but I swear the whole place got a little brighter.

Home for the Holidays

In large mindless herds, recklessly speeding,
forgetting lessons won, heeding poor instincts
at great costs, we, the prodigal lemmings,
find ourselves jetting back, to revisit the cliffs,
with our baggage to exchange season's greetings,

to be rebound by bonds that we once escaped.
Some left through dumb luck, others left through
the clever use of retro-rockets engineered to brake
falling weight, some evolved mutant parachutes,
but we all landed on our feet miles from our fate.

Yet, each year we fall back into step, bearing
our gifts, as we drag reluctant mates and kids
back past the blood-stained crags, not caring
about their fears. Like Pandora, we will unlid
well-wrapped boxes and chests, as if daring
genetics and the past to bring their worst,
because hope always remains like a curse.

American Orpheus

Before he left, they warned
him—the rules are different
down there. Not a single
glance back or one mundane
gesture. A certain shade
of beauty must be ignored.

"Emmett Till, keep them eyes
planted squarely on the ground."

And for his slight indiscretion
he was beaten past the debt
he did not owe, past his youth,
past blackness, past all
suffering into the object
of a modern Passion,
an icon hung on yet
another wall.

Remembering the Body

I think I might convert, become a modern pagan.
The Baltic Perkonis, god of thunder, blesser
of sacred oaks, stern god of my ancestors,
holds a certain ethnic charm. But, I believe
if I stray, I would stagger into the sodden flock
of Bacchus. I could happily attend even biweekly
celebrations of his ecstatic and orgiastic rites.

Imagine a religion founded in the senses.
What sins could its believers commit?
"Father, forgive me for I have remained
chaste and sober for too long." What guilt
could therapists dredge up from the psyches
of humans left alone to enjoy being human?

But when I search my local *Yellow Pages*
for Bacchean Temples, I am confronted
by an absence and forced to reconsider
my more sober faith. I recall how Christ
kept the party at Cana going. How he
commanded others to remember
his body, his blood—the Eucharistic
sacrifice. But what sacrifice could exist
if neither element was not, in some way, joyous?
Once graced with this glimmer of Christ
freed from Gnostic beliefs, I return
to give thanks for the creed
which states that Christ rose
to reign forever, his body restored—
a bright, blood-filled vessel—molded
in the image of the Creator, as are we.

Stroke and Distance:
The Eden Golf and Country Club

Adam made it to 17, a short par 5.
His drive sat square in the middle
of the checker-grained fairway.
His lie was perfect. The Sky Caddie
told him he had 235 left to the green,
215 to the water, 220 to clear the hazard.
As he addressed the ball, preparing
to lay up, a serpent slid between his feet,
coiled around his ball, and looked up
saying, "Go for the green; God does."
Adam stood startled. He had never seen,
let alone named, any species of talking snakes,
but he was even more surprised by the notion
of shooting something other than par.
He never had. There were no handicaps
in paradise. He thought about it,
and asked the snake, "Why?" "Because,
you can." Adam turned, placed his 7 iron
back
    into the quiver and pulled out a 3 wood.
His heart beat in a rhythm he had never heard.
He muscled up, choked the club's grip.
He sped the tempo of his swing. The extra torque
forced him a bit off kilter. He struck the ball
thin, but, having known only success,
he watched it fly with high hopes until it fell
short, dropped in the drink and kicked up
a terrible spray. Adam reached by reflex
to his hip for an extra ball only to realize
that he wore no pants. The serpent slipped
into the rough and laughed like hell,
while the man stood there dead
certain that he would have to pay
some type of penalty.

The Theology of Dodge Ball

Capable of great harm
the jock stands armed
on his side of the court
palming a burnt red ball.
Taking aim he hurls a major
league heater at some nerd's
four-eyed head. As if by miracle,
the kid ducks. Surprised
the poor schmuck standing
behind him begins to realize
that he's the next in line.
He can smell the rubber
closing in, can feel his lips
swell before impact, can hear
the spared laugh, as he goes
down hard. The same game

gets played each summer
around the gulf—depressions
form into storms, enter deep
liquid heat, pick up steam
begin to speed and spin.
Coastal rosaries and prayer
chains snap into action. Prayers
go out to the God of mercy
and compassion, to the creator
of all things on heaven and Earth
to steer this dark agent
of destruction onto another path.

Once the barrage ends, the stricken
will be consoled and told that pain's
the price of playing the game.
The spared will heap praise
on a loving God, as a stained ball
slowly rolls back across a gym floor,

while somewhere out in the tropics
a hot sea heaves and swells.

A Father's Confession

Bless me my children for I have sinned
against you. In your infancy,
I often feigned sleep, listened
to your cries until they roused
your mother who would stumble
into her slippers and then stagger
down the hall and into your rooms.

And I have lied to each of you.
Remember when your t-ball coach
yelled to cover third, so you dove
on the base like a GI covering
a hot grenade, how you refused to move
when the kid on the other team tried
to round the corner? That was not a mistake
that everyone makes. Rudolph never ate
the hay you made me place on the roof.
Santa never downed your eggnog.
Bambi's mother was not shot
with a tranquilizing dart and shipped
to a zoo. Goldfish don't sleep belly up,
nor do they vacation in toilet bowls.
I am not sure that fairy godmothers
or guardian angels actually exist.

For my countless outbursts of anger,
for the time you spent fearing my temper,
for the hours I spent ignoring you as I watched
sports, or sat on this worn green couch
filling notebooks with endless drafts
of forgettable poems, for these transgressions
and for all of those that I have left
unsaid, please know that I am heartily sorry.
Know also that I pray the two of you,
will thrive, find love, and will someday

learn to forgive your father as I learned
to absolve mine, and he did in kind.

Good Enough

In every house of my Slavic aunts
and uncles, the same black and white icon
sat tucked in the gilded frames of copies
of the Last Supper or the Sacred Heart of Jesus,
in the corners of fading photos of Padre Pio
or Pope Paul—a Mass card with a head shot
of the late Catholic president. Too young
in '63, I grew up with no memory of JFK
but I was certain that he was a modern saint
interred beneath an eternal flame.

But then like George and Christopher,
Saint John F's beatification got torpedoed
by stories of his libido and conquests.
But I confess that as a teen, I was mightily
impressed by knowing that the FBI
had tapes of Marilyn and Jack on his bad back
making the bed springs sing—a profile
of endurance indeed, and I began
to cherish the tenet that gives each man
the shot to grab for the last rung of purgatory.

Divine Error

In a Gnostic Gospel, the child
Christ sits playing, molding clay
into life-sized doves. A young
friend looks on as Christ brings
the birds to his mouth. He breathes
life into the clay. Startled into being,
the doves fly off singing praise.

After a small flock had taken wing,
the child sitting next to Christ snapped.
Unable to take anymore of the Son
of Man's divine showing off, he grabbed
a still clay dove and twisted its head
free from its thin neck, and flung
both parts across a small courtyard.
The boy puffed his chest and laughed
as the bird splattered on the hot ground.

Jesus lost control of his human half.
He grabbed his former friend, who felt
the wrath of an angry God pulsing
through him until he, electrified, fell dead.

Mother Mary saw it all. "Jesus
H. Christ! What have you done?"
Jesus didn't have to be omniscient
to know he had stepped into it deep.
Every child understands what it means
when a parent screams a middle name.

By her command and his power,
the playmate was restored. Risen
the confused boy wept, then ran
home, where he waited for his chance
to holler and chant, *Crucify him!*
one Good Friday in Jerusalem.

Why Theology and Economics Don't Mix

As soon as we got back to the car
our father always asked, "So what'chya get?"
Meaning we better produce something
pilfered from the just-visited restaurant.
Doggy bags didn't count, but a shrimp fork,
or juice glass, spoon, napkin, or if nothing
else, packs of sugar or crackers would do.

My mother never played along.
She voiced her disgust, to which Dad
replied, "Ah nuts! It defrays the cost."

I hadn't thought about these petty
thefts for years. Then this Sunday
at Mass, the priest preached on the text
about how the apostles met a stranger
on the road to Emmaus. How they invited
the man to dine with them, and how
it wasn't until the bread had been broken
and the stranger disappeared that they
recognized the Lord. And I began to wonder
just how often Jesus had skipped out on the check.

The Sacrament of Marriage
for Bernerd and Rachael

After the vows are said and the rings
exchanged, know that there will be bad
neighbors who will fill your backyard
with spent beer bottles and disturb
your life with their noise and stereos.

There will be the boring and soul-
numbing jobs, that you will stay in
for the health insurance and the assurance
that the bills will be paid, and the kids
will have what they need
and some of what they want.

There will be short hot arguments
where things that should never
be said will be shouted and screamed.

There will be the small peeves—
drawers left open, seats left up,
the hot curling iron left
in the way of the toothpaste.

There's always a price
for the quiet moment,
the stolen kiss, the cold nights
spent teaspooned together—
those near miraculous moments
when should you be asked
if you still believed that life
was worth it, you'd answer

without thinking, "I do."

from *With Our Baggage*

What I Now Know

What did I know, what did I know...
"Those Winter Sundays," Robert Hayden

We sat for a moment on the metal bench
just this side of security. Her final Christmas
break over, my daughter held on to her photo i.d.
and boarding pass with a diamond adorned hand.

We made small talk when the notion
swept over me like a black wave—she
would not return to be home ever again.
All my past disappointments revisited me.
They poked at bruises and scars as we stood
to hug. The embrace returned me to the side
of my mother's cancer ward bed. My spring
break over, I stood to return to my school life,
my wife and our infant daughter. My mother
reached up and draped her arms around my neck.
She pulled me down toward her with more strength
than I thought she had left. I echoed her affection
and returned her kiss.
                              I regained my balance
in time to watch my daughter merge
into the line of departing passengers.

Born Again: Polish in South Texas

Judging from Juan's face, I shouldn't have said,
"Funny, ain't it? Whenever the diversity committee
brings someone in, they're always Hispanic."

Juan puts down his menu and starts to talk
about the lack of Mexican media role models
and then says, "You Anglos just don't understand."

And I think to myself, *Anglo?* As if
I was not raised on kapusta, kielbasa,
pierogi, and gwumpki, as if

my grandparents had not spoken broken
English at their mill jobs and their
native tongue while at home, as if

as a kid, I did not have to listen to Louey
B. Zigienkowski spin Little Wally polkas
every Sunday on the ride to Mass, as if

the last smart Polack on TV was not
Banacek, played by George Peppard
who really was Anglo, as if ever since

I moved south of the Brazos my history
has been erased—white washed
into that of some tea swilling, scones
eating, Queen loving Englishman.

But Juan is a good friend, and since
we are all guilty of painting the other
with broad strokes, I nod and say,
"Maybe so." I reach across the table
and dunk a corn chip into our salsa.
We sit quietly, reading our menus,
considering our next course.

The Preserver

My office phone rings; some student says
his English teacher gave him my name,
told him I was a real writer. I'm wondering
what new-ex-friend ratted me out. The kid
rambles on, says he needs help; he can't stop
writing; he says, "Words keep flowing like blood
from a deep gash;" this craziness is ruining
his life, consuming him whole, he's at 500
pages and running. "Jesus," I think, "he wants
me to read this thing," but he just keeps talking,
tells me he's not the literary type, reads
the box scores in the paper, that's all,
but now this. He's so scared, he saw
a shrink who asked him about his mother
and gave him pills that put him to sleep.

I ask him what genre he's working in.
I figure if it's prose, I can weasel out.
He says he has no idea what I'm talking
about. I say, "You know is it a story
or a poem?" He says, "It's not like that;
it's more like a universe." He asks
what he should do. I'm stumped,
but I tell him, "Keep writing, this must
be happening for a reason." He thanks me,
but I can sense his desperation as the line
goes dead. I wonder if I did the right thing,
but I think there is a chance that in some new
and slightly askew universe, I am Vishnu,
the Preserver, at least until Shiva shows up
and teaches the kid about second drafts.

The Burden of Genius

Columbo, the unkempt first grader who wears
a slicker rain or shine, is learning that he will
never fit in. Sure there's his eerie glass eye
and those brown patent leather ankle-high boots
that make him stand out, but it's what he notices,
those little inconsistencies in the teacher's
stories that the other kids lap up, that casts
him from the pack. He can't help it if her tales
don't make sense. Take Cinderella, the glass
slippers don't turn back. Everything else
does; and when he points out this fact, the teacher
says, "Frankie, dear, it's only a story." Classmates
turn into parrots and sing, "Frankie dear,"
all day long, so he keeps to himself the idea
that the slippers might not be an error, but a clue.
The whole thing points to another pair of shoes
given beforehand to the prince by the Fairy
Godmother, the two working in cahoots to smooth
a beautiful working girl's sudden rise in status.

Clint Hartung Remembers

All I ever wanted to do was make
a living. It was different back then.
We bought our own cleats and gloves.
We even bought the white socks
that went under the hose. Plumbers
bought their own wrenches, so we
didn't think much of it. When I moved
down here to Sinton to play semi-pro
ball and work for Plymouth Oil, I didn't
take a pay cut. Anyway, no one would know
me now if Mueller hadn't of snapped his ankle
sliding into third. I'm not sure why Leo
sent me into run, but he did, so there
I was taking a lead, and Thompson was up
at bat. He had this hole in his swing;
everyone knew it. He couldn't hit anything
up and in. I mean I might have drilled dry wells
for Plymouth that were smaller, and Branca
threw this good heater up and in, and Bobby
swings, and don't tell me about him having
the signs either, because that's all nonsense.
Anyway, he swings and bingo, all of a sudden
it's blind squirrel and acorn time. The ball
just kept climbing to left, over Pafko, over
the wall, and I was over the moon. I come
down the line skipping and hopping like
some kid in Hondo hearing the circus
is coming to town. National League champs!
And now fifty years later a reporter
for *Sports Illustrated* wants to come down
here and talk to me, and what can I say
except I was just trying to make a living.

Momma Tried

Riding home from Mass
in the back seat next
to my sister, I turned
to her, a pink candy wafer
between my forefinger
and thumb. I said, "The body
of Necco." She smiled,
offered her tongue.

Slap!

My ear rung—burned.
My face blistered red.
Our mother, the nice one,
was screaming in the bottom
of a well through stars,
"You've gone too far!
The sacred is no joke."
My sister's jaw dropped.

This Sunday our priest
low balled the number
of communion wafers
only to be confronted
with an overflow crowd.
He quickly began splitting
each Eucharist into ever smaller
shares until we in the back pew
crowd arrived to receive an ort
of Jesus. Back on our kneeler,
I whispered to my wife, "Body of Christ
my ass. I think I got a big toe."

She laughed. I flinched.

St. Peter's Square 1979

College kids half drunk on cheap spumante,
we decided to stand at the barricades
for hours. As the crowd grew behind us
so did our plan. The new Polish Pope
was returning from Mexico and would pass
within earshot. We knew that he was known
to stop and bless or converse with pilgrims
who spoke his native tongue. Since my mother's
parents came from Poland, the group looked to me,
but my vocabulary was bluer than the Pontiff's
eyes. I feared my broken second-hand Polish
was more likely to land me in the bottom
of some secret and dank Vatican dungeon
than it was to gain us a Papal audience.

Plan B, we decided to consult our foreign language
pocket travel guide. Short of receiving the Paraclete's
gift of tongues, phonetics became our only chance.
We leafed through the little Polish it offered, looking
for some phrase that even Americans could pronounce.
Happy with our choice, we practiced in unison
as if we were again pre-communicants chanting
the *Baltimore Catechism* until we had it right.

That night as the young Pope rode past
a few feet away, we shouted in our best Berlitz,
"Where are you going with our baggage?"

The passing years bent the Pope
in half and hid him behind a cold
plastic mask, but I still relive that night.
Often in a dream, I see his confused look
snap around to our direction, and I swear
I can hear him answer, "Too far, my son, too far."

Skeletons

As a kid I always found it harsh
when my mother claimed that if given
the chance to live her life over,
she'd become a cloistered nun.

My father, an old dog, loved to roll
in life's dirt. One night after I graduated
from high school, my bags packed for college,
he swayed up to me, a fresh Manhattan
sweating and sloshing in his hand. He offered
me slurred advice. "Kid, ya know if I could
do it all over again, I'd been an effing pimp."

After returning from my semester abroad,
I handed out souvenirs. I gave my mom
water from Lourdes, a rosary blessed
by the Pope, and a cheap t-shirt. I brought
my dad brandy from Spain, a Hofbrauhaus
half-liter stein, and second-hand accounts
of his World War II Pig Alley haunts.

My mother enjoyed her gifts, especially
her John Paul II t-shirt. He stood arms raised
and spread, glowing in black and white.
That it was two sizes too large didn't matter
to her. She wore it often and took to saying
again and again, "I can't believe how happy
the Pope looks." My father, who believed
only to a certain point, finally broke one night
during our family meal. To her constant refrain,
he shot back, "For Christ sake, Stella,
I'd be ecstatic too if I had a tit in each hand."
My mother looked down. The Pope looked
up, smiling, her breasts resting in his open palms.
She said nothing. I brayed and snorted, laughing
along with my bent and breathless dad.

A few days later, the shirt appeared, hanging neatly in the corner of my closet. I didn't wear it much, and never in my mother's presence.

Reflection

On Athos the Holy Mountain
the Orthodox monks live their faith.

Pilgrims come. They climb to witness
these men, hoping to catch a glimpse
behind the dark glass. They return

to their day-to-day world changed—
awed by miracles, events the monks
seem not to notice. Some suggest

humility keeps the clerics
from exulting in their works

but, perhaps, to be holy means
to see the miraculous in each step,
each breath of every day.

Resonance

The confessional at St George's
sat on the wing of the altar.
Forgotten in the blueprints,
the parish improvised
and placed a screen and kneeler
in what had been planned to be
a second entrance to the altar.

This meant the priest sat in a corner
of the sacristy which meant nothing
to me until I became an altar boy.
Then I learned that the whispered
admissions of sins echoed off
and were amplified by the church's
stone walls. Waves of guilt bounced
to me as I donned my hassock,
filled cruets with wine and water,
lit the taper to ready the candles.

I tried not to listen, and I easily ignored
the whispered pettiness that occupied
the priest's time and our shared air waves.
But when a real sin resounded off the walls,
I found myself slipping out to the altar
to double check the candles and cruets.
I caught a glimpse of the adulterers,
abusers and users and learned the dowdy
could be desired as much as the beautiful,
the rich felt as burdened as the poor,
and anyone could turn on those they loved.

Good Friday

I once saw my grandmother praying
next to her half turned down
and sagging double bed in her bathrobe
on her ancient knees on a hard wood
floor beneath a humbled deity who bled
oil based paint from chiseled wounds.

Eyes closed she mumbled a mantra
and thumbed her beads—
fingering memories.

She told me once,
"Suffering is a given."

Hope remains
three days away.

from *The Fall of the Leaf*

Introduction

The following poems were written in response to the cello suite *The Fall of the Leaf*, composed by the British composer Imogene Holst in 1964. Imogene Holst unfortunately is better known as the daughter of Gustav Holst and not for her own inventive compositions. I learned of her and *The Fall of the Leaf* when a fellow faculty member at Del Mar College, cellist Susan Sturman, approached me with an idea to collaborate. She had been collaborating with artists in different disciplines to introduce new audiences to modern classical music. She felt *The Fall of the Leaf* deserved a wider audience and could be evocative of poetry. When she asked me, I was pretty uneasy with the notion, mostly because I know nothing about music. But Susan can be quite persuasive. She stressed whatever I wrote could not be wrong, but she wanted me to pay attention that the whole work was written in a minor key except for the last note of the last movement. I googled the significance of minor and major keys soon thereafter and only then had some notion of why that shift in keys might be significant. I listened to a recording of the work for about a month whenever I had a chance. I was also trying to find a clue in the title of the work from which I could write, but what on earth can a poet write about leaves falling that hasn't already been said? As often happens when I'm stuck on something poetic, I turned to Gerard Manley Hopkins. This time I returned to *Spring and Fall*, and all those falling leaves took me to the line: "It is the blight man was born for," which got me to thinking about the fall of man, which gave me the idea that The Fall may have resulted in the first leaves ever to fall and those leaves were the fig leaves Adam and Eve used to cover themselves once they discovered their nakedness. Over the next three months, from June to August, the poems were drafted, and then finished at Duncan Park, an Episcopal retreat center near Ward, Colorado.

I'd like to thank Clarence Wolfshol for his skill and patience in the production of this chapbook, Susan Sturman for conceiving the collaboration from which these poems flowed, Jonathan

Wickham for conversations about these poems in Corpus and Colorado, to Andre (the Intellectual Giant) Rosenbaum de Avillez for conversations about the nature of music which I stole from liberally in these poems, and to my wife, Alice, for her proofreading and putting up with yet another one of my poetic projects.

Part 1: The Fall of the Leaf

Return, as if you could,
to the days of Eden
back before the leaf
or anything else fell,
back to the time
when death,
was just a rumor,

until it wasn't
and Adam and Eve
plucked the first flora
to fall, the fig leaves
that covered
their newfound
nakedness,

and ask if the leaves
were not wasted
in the fashioning
of bras and G-strings

and if fedoras and neckties
would not have made
more sense? For we
all know, the root
of what sin there is
always stems from deep
within the human
mind and heart.

Part 2: Brokenness

Ever since the second bite
  we have been taught
  that all was broken:

broken as a crystal glass
  on a marble floor,

broken as a bone
  in an Inquisitor's vice,

broken as a child
  cowering from a
  broken parent
    breaking bonds and trusts
    that should never be broken,

broken as the soul
  where all belief is lost.

All of this loss for the want
  of a better snack
an unpalatable creed
  that's so hard to swallow.

Every millennium or two
a prophet appears to remind
Eden's heirs that answers
and grace, hard won, still exist
deep within each being's skin
waiting for those willing to dive
deep, waiting for us to understand
answers are never consumed
or found in low hanging fruit.

Part 3: The Mystic Within

Upon commissioning these poems,
the cellist said, "No worries.
Just write like Rumi,"
and sauntered off,
never turning back
to see the weight of Rumi's
genius buckle me, crushing
the possibility of poetry.

I mean what are the chances
this bent modern cynic
could write like an ancient mystic?
Hell, when you think about it,
Rumi didn't even write left to right.

Given time, I calmed down
and thought about Rumi
and his art, his Beloved
and sight beyond the eye
that penetrates the heart

and I realized the only man
who might have believed
that I could write like Rumi
would have been Rumi himself.

Graced with this insight,
I turned on the glow
of my once-bitten Apple
and commenced to typing
one one-thousandth
of a picture at a time.

Part 4: The Music

Musicians tell me that music
consists of these printed dots
and symbols I cannot fathom.

Music historians and philosophers
counter, saying that before Edison,
before his recordings, sheet music
was no more than a guide
for each unique performance,
but now with the need to replicate
the frozen ideals trapped
in an audience's mind,
the music on the page died.

To a poet, like the dancer and the dance
the lover and the beloved, the music
and the cellist are one. The score's sight-read
then given life through skill and talent,
wrought through decades of dedication.
Her fingers coax the music out as she strokes
and plucks tuned strings that vibrate,
amplified by a body of caressed maple.

The produced waves flow out to the audience
who sit in anticipation of the next note,
pleased and surprised by the pattern
that pulses past them one undulation
at a time. Each wave rolls out beyond
the seats until the very air that sustains
the waves erodes them into nothingness.

Friction's the birth and death of music,
or is it? For Physics claims everything
that is seen and unseen is made of strings,
and each string differing in size
and function, from the subatomic

to those strings that cross galaxies
and dimensions. Everything
consists of strings and all strings
vibrate, so perhaps each note,
each wave set loose here tonight
will reverberate forever in our cores,
leaving all that have been washed
in their wake more vibrant and attuned.

Part 5: Practicing Resurrection

When the fabric rends—
the shots go off
the plane dives
into the ocean
or a sea of glass—
we throw fists
and invective
toward a smugly
placid sky,
join in unison
the plaintiff cry
"Why?"

demanding
signs and answers
while each day
the miracle
of the fabric itself—
the plane that lands
the couple that loves
the masses that follow
the Golden Rules—
goes unnoticed

as do the good souls
who work to darn
the breaches
and by doing so
sow once again
our patchwork
world reborn.

Atlas Sighs: new poems

Angling with D.H. Lawrence

As an undergraduate I was first drawn to him
by the short introduction in our anthology
that described him as the son of a refined woman
and a lout, our shared biography in a nutshell.

The Junior Poet Project was the bane
of English majors at my Catholic school.
We were to pick one of Norton's poets,
learn the poetry, the biography, the criticism
and then sit for an hour or more
to be grilled by a panel of PhD's.

The good students in their need
to impress selected the expected,
Dickinson, Donne, Browning, Auden,
Yeats, Keats, Eliot, and Hopkins
of course. Poets the faculty knew well
and could recite by their iambic-beating hearts.

But there are advantages, be they but a few,
of being sired by a lout. My old man's
greatest lesson came to mind: "Angles,
Son, the secret is to always find the angle."

I figured my chances for success lay
in the areas of the faculty's ignorance,
so I studied the ignored D. H. Lawrence,
his understated diction, his debt to Whitman,
his search for blood knowledge, wisdom
not gained but found, found at the moment
of climax. And it worked. I made one of two A's,
made an A studying a pagan's theory of sex
at a Catholic U—now how's that for a ricochet?

But the biggest payoff came way down the road,
on a first date with a woman out of my league

but on the rebound. As we sat at the movies
watching the always prowling Captain Kirk
recite lines of poetry to his target—a perky
marine biologist, "They say the sea is cold,
but the sea contains the hottest blood of all."
I leaned to my date's ear and whispered,
"That's from D.H. Lawrence's 'Whales Weep Not.'"
Seconds later the projected and impressed
biologist repeated what I had just whispered
for all to hear, and, for that one glorious moment,
the desired woman seated to my right, thought,
"I'll be damned, kind of ugly but really smart!"

Even though I proved her theory wrong
a thousand times over, we remain long wed,
and I'm still grateful for the secrets of fire
taught by blood, so I offer this hymn of praise—

God bless David Herbert Lawrence, ricochets,
rebounds, and every angle well played.

How The Adventurer in Me Died Behind 5 Bars

I held out for years. "But you
drive so far to work, what if
you breakdown or have a flat?"
my wife would say. "In 1492
Columbus sailed the ocean blue
without a cellphone," I'd reply.

"I'm sure your random knowledge
of heroic couplets and bad actors
will come in handy in the middle
of nowhere should you have a wreck
on those backroads you take," she'd scoff.
"Life is a grand adventure, and I'm off,"
I'd shout and head for the door.

But somewhere along the line
as my testosterone levels waned
her refrain morphed into common sense,
so now I live under the safety of a net-
work of cell towers strewn across
the desolate south Texas landscape,
and I keep roadside support programmed
into speed dial just in case, just in case...

Why Barry Bonds Belongs in Cooperstown

Baseball writers and afficionados
have banned Bonds to infamy.
They say, "He cheated; it was the juice
that slammed 73 in ought-one."

If so, I might be the Barry Bonds
of the Sinton Municipal Golf Course
thanks to the injections of steroids
prescribed by my GP, a good golfer
in his own right. At 63 I am bombing
the ball farther than back in my prime.

The ball is slicing way farther to the right,
and duck hooking harder to the left; it goes deeper
into the trees, and into deeper water.
The ball now sizzles off the club face,
whistles an age-old song, "There's no
prescription that cures a lack of talent.
There's no substitute for well-honed skill."

The Theology of a Weekend Golfer

for Robert Oman & Ray Schroeder

My golfing buddy Bob mutters,
"It's just a hobby," after he
occasionally shanks a shot
before he trudges a few yards
up the fairway or ventures
out into the thick rough.

Bob plays by the rules, believes
all the stuff the golfing great
and fervent Baptist, Bobby Jones
preached about playing the ball
where it lies and how golf reveals
character. But I've never bought

into the idea that a game could mean
so much. Especially a game whose rule book
was written by a clan of Georgian Scots.
I see Calvin's heavy thumb on every page.

Some would say I cheat, but, due to my
fallen nature, do I have a choice?
Not that I think it matters. For I believe
in a loving and forgiving God who gladly
doles out infinite second chances.

I bump my ball to improve my lie,
walk it away from trees and roots
to protect my wrists and clubs.
I keep my pockets full of balls,
so when the shank invariably comes,
I can throw down a second ball
and retake the shot. If that ball
by some miracle gets closer to the hole,
that's the one I play. If a ball finds the water,
I keep hitting balls until one finds dry land.

Penalty strokes? Come on, at four bucks
a pop, drowning balls is penalty enough.

What's that? Did I hear you say
that's not fair to Bob or our friend Ray,
Ray who knows where his ball is going
every damn time the man swings?
Perhaps, but we never play for stakes.
I don't have a card the PGA can take.
I never turn in a scorecard to establish
a handicap, don't have to according to Ray,
who says my swing is handicap enough.
So I ask, what's the harm in taking a few
mulligans? After all, golf's just a hobby.

Total Immersion

For Richard Whatley & Boyd Tyndall

My friend Richard, now in his 80's,
finally retired from his furniture store.
A Baptist to the core, he called me
late on a weekday night, stone sober,
auditioning, if you will, to be a character
in some future poem that I *should* write.

He reminded me of the time we were on eight,
a short par three over water that always plays
into the wind, how I had got lucky and landed
my tee shot a few feet from the pin, how as I walked
to the green a gale force gust of wind caught
my pushcart, how it picked up speed all on its own,
how it headed straight for the pond and then
how it flew like Evel Knevel did in Vegas,
that time Evel jumped the fountain at Caesars Palace,
but once my unmanned cart launched
it flew more like a wounded duck with my wallet
and cell phone riding in the attached golf bag,
how it splashed down in the pond's middle,
and how I had to jump in and wade out
into the chest high gunk before it sunk,
and then soaking wet and barefoot how I missed
my short birdie putt, how I went home
mad, sad, and sodden, and if that story
won't do maybe I could write about the time
on the same hole, how our friend Boyd
who is a mountain of a man tried to hit
his ball out of the water at the pond's edge
and ended up looking like the Swamp Thing.

Richard says he's sure these poems
would be hits. I tell him I have my doubts,
but Richard reminds me he's a can-do-
kind of guy and says all he can do is try.

I pass on the crack about him being trying,
stunned by how much the entry
into literary obscurity means to him.

After the call ended, I jotted down
some notes, and to my surprise,
I started to see that Richard
just might get his wish.

The Legends of the Ring

One day before my wife's dual credit
English class began, a polite student
raised her hand, and asked Alice
if she was related to the Berecka
who golfs at the Sinton course.
When Alice said yes, her husband,
the young woman went on to say
that her folks once ran the clubhouse
out there and when she was just a toddler,
she helped saved the teacher's marriage.

She added how she still remembers the day
he lost his wedding ring, after it flew off
his sweat-soaked finger as he followed
through with a five iron on the fourth hole,
how he and his buddies looked for hours
for the missing ring, how her mother
even lent them her metal detector
but to no avail, and then near closing time,
as the sun began to sink into the tops
of the old live oaks and her mother drove
a cart over to check on the golfers' quest,
while the girl dawdled riding shotgun
until she happened to notice a glint in the grass,
how she yelled at her mother to stop the cart,
and then bingo! The student got a bit emotional
as she recalled how she ran and picked up the ring.

Alice thanked her for her efforts and story,
but the thing is Alice remembers that day
and how I panicked on the fourth green
after I sank a putt and looked down
at my ringless left hand, how a sick feeling
flashed through me and the memory
of how once when we were just married
the ring had slid off inside my ball mitt,

how I panicked when I finally noticed its absence
but then found it nestled halfway down
a leather finger as I sat at a bar drinking
with teammates, how vividly that memory
then replayed in my head as I explained
to my fivesome that the ring, which I wear
but was my paternal grandfather's first,
must have slid off when I took off
my golf glove somewhere back in the fairway.
She knows we searched for hours, that we
even used a borrowed metal detector
and the clubhouse crew checked in on us often
but she also knows I went home ringless, confessed
to her my carelessness and how relieved
I was when her reaction was better than I expected.

Alice knows I then climbed the stairs and went
into our bedroom to gather up some after-shower wear,
and there sitting on my dresser was the gold wedding ring
that I had forgotten to put on that day. Alice
can still hear my scream, "Oh my God, it's here!"

That evening, I phoned my friends and told them the news,
which over a decade on they have yet to let me live down.
As I tee up on the fourth tee box, one of them might say
"Careful, Alan, I hear there's leprechaun guarding gold
on this hole." I also know the day ended with me relieved
and refreshed back out at the clubhouse, where the lights
were about to be turned off. I entered with my ring
to apologize and walked into a parallel universe.

If You Can't Beat'em...

They argued often, she trying to convince
him that what he thought he saw
made no sense, but logic was lost on him.

Faye grew tired of the fights, and gave up hope
that Ben's brain set asea by a high tide
of fluids would ever come up for a breath
of sanity, so she decided to dive headlong
into the absurd and swim with her frail spouse.

One day when he screamed, "Faye, Faye,
come quick!" as he stared out the window,
"Look, there's four Franciscans riding buffaloes."
Exasperated, she sidled over and replied,
"No, Ben, you're wrong. I count five."

At which point to her surprise and relief,
he went quiet while counting the clergy-
driven herd again and again, wondering
where the other buffalo had roamed.
He sighed, "Are you sure?" "Oh yeah,
five for sure, maybe six." He sat quietly
the whole afternoon, as if on a safari,
waiting for his vision to be complete,
and she wondered if she should feel
guilty, thought she might go to confession
if one of those friars ever dismounted.

The Crack...

...*it's how the light gets in.*
Leonard Cohen

It was Thursday, a school night,
but I was up at a quarter to midnight,
sitting close to our murky color TV,
so I could keep its volume down
not wanting to stir my parents
from their drunken slumbers.

Too young to remember the glory years,
although I once saw the likes of Berra
and DiMaggio trot out on Old Timer's Day,
too young to remember Mantle
with two good legs, I grew up
rooting for the likes of Jake Gibbs
and Horace Clark in Yankee pinstripes.

So when Brett hit a tying 3 run homer
off of Jackson in the top of the ninth
on that cold October night, I knew Littell
was a cinch to send the game to extras
where the Yanks were sure to lose the series,
lose like every other team I ever rooted for.

But then Chris Chambliss swung
at the first pitch, cracked a line drive
over McCrae's head, over the wall
in right center, and the fans poured
onto the field as I jumped to my feet,
screamed in joy. As Chambliss bulled
his way through the riot back to home plate,
I moved back, sat down on a worn couch,
watched the mayhem through unexpected tears
and was confused by the palpable sense
that my life might hold far-flung possibilities.

The Knock Answered

Communion for us was spiritual
Russian Roulette, and at best
practiced once or twice a year.

If given the choice, my clan went
to confession right before Mass;
if given the chance, we would
confess directly before the flock
lined up at the altar railing
lest an impure thought enter
our heads and sully the host's
grace—derail our salvation
and cement our damnation.

My college dorm senior year
also housed the school's chaplain
Father Fischer, who we called
the Fish, an RFK look-alike.
One day he rapped on my door.
Surprised to see a rock star priest
standing there, I drowned in an instant
sea of guilt, figured he had come
to excommunicate this horndog of a sinner.

He stepped in the room, said he
wanted to ask me a question.
I thought I would hear something
like "Who do you think you are
pretending to be a Christian?"
But instead he asked, "So I see you
at Mass nearly every week; why
don't you take communion? After all
son, it's like going to the opera
and not hearing the music."

I tried to explain my unworthiness
tried to tell him I hadn't confessed
in quite a while. He smiled and said
"Ah, I see, you think Jesus Christ
died for everybody's sins but yours?
Kind of egotistical don't you think?"
I winced; he nodded knowingly.
"I'll see you in the communion line
Sunday then?" I felt a weight lift
and have been grateful ever since.

Vilnius Pilgrimage: First Steps

One Sunday in Vilnius
while others looked for God
in ancient rites and rituals,
I searched for Frank Zappa.

I hope the faithful
had more luck than me
as Zappa's statue remains
a rumor, and all I have
are secondhand accounts
and newfound doubts.

Vilnius Pilgrimage: Course Correction

Today I found Frank Zappa,
his giant granite head
mounted on a stainless
steel column, his bust
looking like the work
of the mad Vlad the Impaler
had Vlad mounted heads
on blunted stainless pikes.

Although on the correct street,
I now know I had not walked
far enough, was not looking
in the right direction, that I
completely missed the signs,

so sure was I that Zappa
belonged in a park, not in
something resembling
an abandoned parking lot,
my preconceptions keeping
me from finding the father
of the Mothers of Invention.

The Tourist's Dilemma

Once your feet begin to blister,
you only have two choices.

You can sit in your hotel room
and let your sores heal,
and, by doing so, miss
the sights you came to see,

or you can trudge on
try to ignore the pain
and soak in the sights
as each step digs deeper
into the soft flesh
on your heels and soles.

The Only Basket in Town

350 miles away, as the crow flies, much more
if you measure by the course of a butterfly,
each wing flap of which in theory can change

the world, Russian missiles are falling
on the children of Ukraine, as I sit
in Vilnius a half-day's drive from Kiev

watching the only channel in English
I can find, CNN International, as they
cover a war that feels a world away.

Outside my window a cold rain falls.
Umbrellas up, eyes straight ahead,
Lithuanians go about their business.

They know to their east the word Czar
morphed from Caesar, and emperors
need their empires. Putin is nothing
new. What's new is NATO membership,

and every egg these stoics own, be it chicken,
crow or butterfly, is carried gingerly in that one
basket. To show support for Kiev, they've dyed

these eggs yellow and blue, as they hope
this time something in the world has changed
and the eggs won't be squashed or stained red.

Hearing of Uvalde while Visiting Vilnius

I saw a woman from Italy begin to weep
as she walked through the basement
cells beneath the KGB museum.
"Overwhelmed, just overwhelmed,"
she said, "by the inhumanity
of it all." Overwhelmed in a foreign land,
overwhelmed forty years after the fact.

I do not tell her I come from Texas,
South Texas so near to Uvalde
where children at school, children
at school were gunned down.

I cannot explain how it is possible
for me to walk or even stand today,
cannot explain why I am not wearing
sackcloth and ashes, how could I explain
that I come from a country that loves guns
more than life, a land where even our worst
tragedies just leave us numb.

Wings not Feathers, Emily

On moonless summer nights,
hope flitters then darts in front
of us blinking bright neon green,
seemingly just out of reach,
but then captured in the cup
of our childlike hands
and placed in mason jars,
filling the night with magical light.

Hope captured does not last.
The morning after finds
entwined corpses of fireflies
a gross mass which we toss
from glass to grass,
but, ah, then comes
the cool summer night.

Lighten Up

You don't have to be Atlas
to know this world is a heavy place.

If the meek be blessed, I ask
what of the belligerent, the alpha dogs
who bite and claw, stepping on others
all the way to what they see as success,
unburdened by pangs of conscience?

By adding to the burden, piling on,
they do nothing more than aid gravity's
mindless force that crushes the life
out of all of us a bit quicker
than it would leave on its own.

No, I believe the real trick, the only true
human accomplishment, is to make the world
a lighter place. Start small, pat a slouching back,
hand out a compliment, dry a tear, share a smile,
or a laugh, create some art, lift a soul,
even if it's just your own, or better yet,
let your work reach a friend or two,
or go all out like the saints, open
your heart wide, feed the hungry,
cure the sick, visit the lonely,
befriend justice and reap
the blessings, listen
for the sigh
of Atlas.

Restoration

with warm breast and with ah! bright wings.
Gerard Manly Hopkins

Reading to Catholic sixth graders,
I realize too late that a confession
of doubt about the existence
of guardian angels might draw
a shocked gasp from the font
of innocence long forgotten
by my ilk of dry cynic.

I worry I have caused long term
harm, but then watch as they recover
to wade into penning their own poetry
with callous-free fingers raised in the air
as they count and recount syllables—

five, seven, and five,
then break into white-winged smiles
of haiku success.

Regressive
Thoughts
on Infinity

Driving cross this country on I-10
at the Texas-Louisiana border
the green sign says El Paso
857 miles; I think,
if it's not turtles
it has to be
Texas all
the way
down

. .

.

Hey Abbooooott!!!!
(Lou Costello)

Funny ain't it, that in this state
that still enforces Blue Laws
for booze on Sundays, in this state
where gamblers have to hightail it
over the state line to feed eight liners,
in this state where marijuana
is still illegal for most purposes,
in this state where reproductive rights
are being eroded quicker than our coast,
in this state that doesn't even trust
its citizens to vote, our governor claims
that wearing a mask to curtail COVID
is a matter of personal responsibility,
which has me hoping that any day
now, I'll be able to light a joint
and swig a beer at my local casino
early on some fine Sunday morning,
but, should these hopes prove false,
perhaps our governor might decide
to stop out-Trumping DeSantis as he
illegally gambles with so many lives.

Gravity

There's always the pull
of inanimate things—

the rattle and pacifier in our cribs,
the counsel of a stuffed bear,

the gold star on grade school papers,
the monogramed lettermen's jacket,

the dreams of Eden engendered
with each lottery ticket bought,

there's the freedom hinted at by exhaust
wafting from a new car's tailpipe,

until the payment comes due
and the insurance gets hiked.

How strong those must be,
those who reverse this tide,

those who slip out to deserts,
or sit beneath the bodhi, but even they…

I know of a man, a gifted poet,
educated to the max, he took

odd jobs, worked for room and board,
worked for just enough, enough

to wall himself away from the world
and write his poems every day.

In the end, the poet turned bitter.
The world never noticed his brilliance

never stormed the wall he erected
to offer him its acclaim and riches.

So few are the saints that escape
the basic rule of the physical world:

The gravity of inanimate things
always pulls toward disappointment.

Doing the Conga

Time management
is an industry
built on a lie,

unless travelling
at the speed of light,
or in H.G. Wells'
contraption, time
remains unbridled,

with its constant
beat, the tick-tock
of the cosmic
conga line,
each beat
an invitation
to join in

step, step
step, step
out, shout!

each step,
a celebration

until the dancers
exhausted can do
nothing more
but lie down
and sleep.

Haunted

I wish it was a vague memory
of that one Halloween, when my older
sister and cousin, Cookie and Tootsie
hatched the plan to parade around
costumed as an untalented living
negative of a popular pop trio.

Younger and defenseless, I became
the third white Supreme. I squeezed
into a dime store faux evening gown.
I left my aunt's under a plastic wig,
a pint-sized drag queen, festooned
in red rouge and bright lipstick.

At each house, we eschewed the normal
trick or treat, raised our right palms
and launched into our lines, "Stop!
In the name of love, before you break
my heart; Think it o-o-ver," in some
atonal key,
        then stood there anxiously
as some slightly shocked if not awed
homeowner we had taken off guard
forked over gobs of candy.
                            Long before
worries of cultural appropriation,
in the Polish and Irish Westend of town
we made a haul, but looking back,
thinking it over,
                    I confess that I have
never felt comfortable in a costume again,
like some stain from that night,

the sense of something
                            not quite
being right,
            keeps on
                        hanging on.

The Day Music was Placed on Life Support

In the fourth grade, still eager to please,
I went to choir tryouts, not knowing
what to expect of the teacher, aptly named
Mrs. Batty, who asked what I would like to sing.

My mind shifted into overdrive, as I reviewed
the few tunes I knew. There was Frankie Yankovic's,
"She's too Fat for Me," and "Who Stole the Kishka?"
but I figured those wouldn't fly; after all,
one was too mean, the other made no sense.
I mean someone might want to steal
a kielbasa, but a kishka? Come on,
a blood sausage? Only Aunt Rita could eat
those things, hardly a mystery Frankie,
no need for Columbo to solve that one,
but Mrs. Batty still sat on her piano bench
impatiently waiting for my answer,
and only one other song kept coming to mind,
one that was playing constantly on WTLB,
the rock of the Mohawk Valley, so I blurted
"Ruby, Don't Take Your Love to Town."

I stumbled a bit through the first verse:
"You've painted up your lips and rolled
and curled your tinted hair. Ruby,
are you contemplating going out somewhere?"

But when the chorus came, I did my best
Kenny Rogers in the First Edition
impersonation, sucked in air to hit
the low notes. I went so low I risked
contracting the bends, so low that Tibetan
throat singers would've envied the depth,
that is, if Buddhist monks from Tibet
are capable of envy. I didn't make it through
the next verse: "It wasn't me that started

that old crazy Asian war…" when Mrs. Batty pretty much screamed, "Enough, enough!"

I looked at her expectantly, knowing my place on the risers was secure. She composed herself, and said, "Son, do me, yourself, and the world a favor; never, ever, sing in public again. Next."

How the Lion in Me Died

After Butkus and Unitas hung up
their cleats, Lithuanian kids
didn't have many jocks to root for
except for the tennis great Vitas Gerulaitis
with his blonde mane, the Lithuanian Lion
who roamed the courts, and nightclubs—
a blazing Baltic star that placed a cheap
Wilson metal racket in my hand.

Junior year I took my act to school
and the tennis team tryouts.
There were ten of us, the process
was going to be easy, a tournament
top six would be on the team.
I finished fourth, not bad—
good enough; after all, my hero
had peaked at world number three.

Until I read the names posted
on the bulletin board the next day.
Mine wasn't there. Confused,
I sought out the coach, who told me
in the most casual of ways
he had not expected anyone
on last year's team to lose,
figured they did because they
had a bad day; besides, he confessed,
the parents of the kid who finished
next to last owned the court we played on.

Unfair I suppose, but when I got home
and complained, my worn father
shrugged and welcomed me
to his universe, a place so cold
that a few years in the future
the Lion himself would lose his life

thanks to the toxic fumes given off
by a faulty guesthouse heater.

The Romantic in Me Died at Rock Bottom

The Bee Gees started asking
their question when I was in middle school,
but junior year in college when a girlfriend
showed me an engagement ring
I hadn't bought, the old song
became oddly relevant: "How do you
(Alan Berecka) mend a broken heart?"

After some trial and error and a bit of research,
I believed I had stumbled, well more like
swayed then staggered, onto the answer—
For three months each night I drank
a pint or two of Mad Dog 20/20
poured into a cheap plastic tumbler
filled with ice, and then I slammed
down anything else I could drink.

A dumb kid with grades and life in a deathroll,
rock bottom hit me as I lay on my back
crash-landed on a bench just after
I projectile vomited a volcano's worth
of hot semi-digested wine skyward.

I was failing physics that semester
but I knew a few of Newton's
basic rules. I had the time
but was unable to move.

Splash down came:
lined my glasses
filled my nose,

blind and gasping
worse off than a fish out of water,
it was then I began to realize the morass
I floundered in amounted to nothing

more than pathetic and useless pining,
and thanks to reality's hot slap
to the face, I started a long and often
unsuccessful courtship with sobriety.

The Malicious Rabbit and Raisin Cookies:
An Apology for Timeout

She wanted our first married dinner to be just right;
I promised myself it would be as I feigned constant delight.

Since her mother was to blame for these awful recipes,
why should I risk sex or happiness (or sex) on matters culinary?

We did just fine until the final course when her offering shook me.
Good God, there they were—home-baked raisin cookies!

As I paled to contemplate a night (hell, a whole life) without nookie
(no monk I), still I declined those awful morsels offered so sweetly.

"But why?" she demanded. "I promise they aren't burned."
"It's not you, it's my dark past; so listen if you dare and learn.

Before timeout, desperate mothers improvised frequently
as my own did that day I committed some toddled felony.

She said, 'Tomorrow's Easter; the bunny's coming, you know?'
'So?' Unimpressed, I was a pint-sized hood on parole.

'I'm warning you son, bad boys don't get sweets, just bunny
kupies.'" My wife smiles, "Some kind of Polish treat?"

"No, it's Polish for excrement." Her napkin fell from her lap.
"Yes dear, in bad boys' baskets the Polish bunny is known to crap

or so my mother claimed, but wise for my age, I wasn't buying.
Pushing my mother's sanity, her patience I kept trying.

I pushed too far; something snapped; my parole soon ended.
The next morning my older sister who had always been offended

by the fact that I had been born, gladly aided
in my sentence, so my hand in hers we paraded

dressed in our Sunday finest to find our holiday wicker.
The white chocolate bunny caught my eye, but something sicker

there my wicked sister pretended to happily find:
little wrinkled dried black things. Can't be, cried my mind.

My sister smiled, then she slipping past the absurd
picked one up and asked, 'Ever taste a real bunny turd?'

'They ain't half bad except for the smell'; slipping it past
her smiling teeth, she slowly chewed her macabre repast.

My stomach churned, my head spun like Linda Blair's
then suddenly my semi-digested breakfast reappeared.

'You're so gross!' my sister screamed,
and my mother apologized for being mean.

As my mother changed my clothes, she explained what she had done,
but to this day, dear, there has never been a raisin in her son."

That night we went out for ice cream; I had hot fudge.
These days when our kids act up, from the couch they don't budge.

Tex Mex Food 101

Mexican bakeries
in South Texas
sell it by the slice

I could eat it
by the ton—
white pound cake

iced in thick
pink frosting
that hints

of a tang
of citrus.
The perfect

mix of tastes
that even
this gringo

can order
in the local
Spanish dialect,

as I point
and ask for
"Pink Cake!"

and think
to myself,
Gracias a Dios.

Coastal Advice

Chlorophyll from
microscopic plankton
unseen and suspended
in its sheltered waters
turns Corpus Christi
Bay a pale emerald
green year round,
astounds and worries
the tourists who
having seen the refineries
wonder if it's toxic being
so used to thinking
water needs to be blue,
but locals tell them
thinking is overrated
and they just need
to relax and dive in.

A Prayer as Dorothy Goes Marching Out
for Dorothy Alexander

Little sister there are no more
storms to chase, no more
cases to try, no more
rulings to rule,
no more poems to pen,
the good fight in a red hat
has been fought past the bell

nothing to do now but return
to the corner, let us bind
your wounds, untie your gloves
unwrap your fists. Relax
little sister and slip
between the ropes
into nothingness.

But to my surprise, should you
continue beyond the page, please,
find me a loophole and pull me through.

Revising Butler's *Lives of the Saints*

Saint Patrick, the great shooer
of snakes, patron saint of Ireland,
Nigeria, and civil engineers, immortal
being that he is, seems to be stuck
in the past, so I suggest from now on
he also become the patron of all consumers
of shamrock shakes and green beer,
and any other uncivil revelers who keeps
his feast marked on their calendars
and needs his help to survive
its sodden hours more than
any sober engineer ever might.

Alarming

Wake the hell up, will ya!
my old man's voice and anger
often grounded my mind's flights
of fancy, returned me to the real
world and some assigned chore.

The state of awake-ness to him
was the core of a blue-collar ethos,
was the height of being, it meant
you cared enough to care, it meant
you wanted to get things right.

So to my friends who prefer to slumber
in the certainty of the Dark Ages,
before Galileo and the likes shook
the universe up, I plead as calmly
as I can: Please, wake the hell up!

Mrs. Robinson Forgets Joe DiMaggio

Where have you gone
Walter Cronkite?

Our nation turns its
bleary eyes to you.

We long to know "The way
it is" once more. Please,

show us the way back
to a country united under one

set of facts. Help us recall facts differ
from opinions, both yours and mine.

Remind us again that Jesus loves us
all more than any of us can know.

We look to you Uncle Walter
to revive our gasping body politic

unresponsive turning blue on the floor.
Breathe back life into the common good

our one nation once united
by more than the vainest

of notions, our new and fallen creed—
"Yeah, but, what's in it for me?"

What's that you say Mrs. Robinson?
Uncle Walter's left and gone away.

Hey, hey, hey.
Woe, woe, woe.

A Transplant Speaks

My wife has no talent for horticulture.
Every gifted plant she ever received
found itself on death row, condemned
to wither to a slow death, executed
by what she calls her *black thumbs.*

I grew up in a verdant northern valley
beneath ancient pines and maples.
Recently, I entered a confused state
caused by a sort of identity crisis
brought on by an invitation to submit
to an anthology of Southern writers.

Nonplussed, my wife, once a military brat,
who was born in South Dakota from folks
who called Missouri home but ended up in Dallas,
told me, "Do the math. For two-thirds of your life,
you have lived in Texas." She reminded me
that I studied at its universities and added
that we met and were married in Texas,
that our children were born and raised here,
that we have decided to retire and stay here
and asked, "So why shouldn't you be a Texan?"

A few years back, my wife brought home
a few hopeless-looking green sticks.
"They're Plumeria," she claimed, placing
them each in its own large ceramic pot.
I laughed, but in spite of their presumed fate
the sticks flourished, bloomed, and multiplied.
Our back patio now resembles a flowering forest.

Shallow root systems promote successful
transplantations, an accident which can allow
the answer to "Where do you live?" and "Where
are you from?" to merge painlessly. As for me,

a lost son of rural Central New York, who wears
a worn Yankee cap most days, I guess I need
to face some basic facts like I no longer own
a snow shovel and find a bit more gratitude
for this sun-drenched place that I have lived
in for so long that *y'all* has gently nudged
yuz guys from my everyday speech.

Of Spiritual Storms and Ports
For my All Saints Family

I never heard my parents' questions
but the priest, a burly and unkempt
Franciscan, always answered the same:
"I can tell you what the church says, but
God gave you a brain and a conscience,
so don't fret. I trust you, and so does He."

In college, curiosity led me a to class
on the liturgy. The hard-living Irish priest,
a scholar who had written parts of *Vatican II,*
recited Hopkins by rote to illustrate
the finer points of the sacramental essence
of the universe. More than once, he'd go pale
grab his chest, and tell a seminarian to run
and retrieve his nitro pills from his office.
When the excitement passed, he'd whisper
in a croaky brogue, "Boys, if you learn
one thing from this class, understand
Catholicism practiced correctly is descriptive
not prescriptive like every other religion.
For example, we use wine not grape juice
at communion because that joyous buzz
from a good belt of wine is a precursor
of the joys we can find through the Lord
in his kingdom where the buzz will last
forever and ever without end. Amen."

But somewhere along the way, the church's
pews grew harder and cold. I broiled at sermons
that became roll calls for a morality-police squad
whose marching orders were to go back
into the world and keep score by counting
all the must-do's and not-do's that added up
to certain salvation or damnation.

While I was doing a poetry workshop
at a beyond progressive Episcopal church,
someone asked me what flavor of believer
I was. I thought for a second and answered,
"A disgruntled Catholic, I suppose."

The priest, who moonlighted as a poet
replied, "Why fret? Join us, same cookie,
less guilt." When I learned Jesus bled
port there on Sundays, the deal was sealed.

About the Author

Alan Berecka, the grandson of four immigrants from Eastern Europe, a son of Albert and Stella and Central New York, brother of Janis, proud alum of Holland Patent Central High— the University of Dallas—UNT—TWU, the husband to and admirer of Alice for nearly four decades, the father to Rachael and Aaron, a former poet laureate of Corpus Christi, a longtime resident of Sinton, Texas, a retired librarian, an avid but no more than average golfer, has written some poems along the way which other folks chose to put in dozens of periodicals, anthologies, chapbooks, and five other books. He has travelled throughout the US and twice to Lithuanian to read at festivals and be featured at literary events. Berecka is grateful for the strangely wonderful life he has led, and the friends and folks that have made it so remarkable.

Acknowledgments

The selected poems come from four collection: *The Comic Flaw*, (NeoNuma Arts: Houston, 2008), *Remembering the Body* (Mongrel Empire Press, Norman, OK, 2011), *With Our Baggage* (Lamar University Press, Beaumont, TX, 2013), and the limited run chapbook *The Fall of the Leaf* (El Grito del Lobo Press, Fulton, MO, 2017). In creating this collection, the decision was made to include poems from full collections that were at least 10 years old. In doing so, two more recent collections were excluded. An exception to the 10-year rule was made for *The Fall of the Leaf* because it has been sold out and unavailable for some time.

I would like to thank Neil Orts, publisher, and Jill Alexander Essbaum Peng, editor, of *The Comic Flaw*, Jeanetta Calhoun Mish, editor of *Remembering the Body*, Jerry Craven, editor of *With Our Baggage*, and Clarence Wolfshohl, editor and master printer who helped create *The Fall of the Leaf*. Poems in the selections from these collections appeared in journals such as *The Windhover, Slow Trains, The Penwood Review, The Windward Review, The Red River Review, The Texas Review, Ardent, The Blue Rock Review, The Christian Century, The San Antonio Express, Concho River Review*, and in the anthology *St. Peter's B-List: Contemporary Poems Inspired by the Saints* (Ave Maria Press).

Poems in the New Poems were published in the *Langdon Review of Arts in Texas, The Texas Poetry Assignment, The Corpus Christi Writers Anthology, Concho River Review*, and the anthology *Southern Voices* (Lamar University Press).

My gratitude and thanks to all who have given their time to this project, including Joey Brown, Hank Jones, Larry D. Thomas, Ken Hada, and especially the editor, Paul Bowers, who is so patient he makes Job look anxious.

The greatest gift the practice of poetry brings is friendships with fellow poets and readers. Many thanks to all of you. And finally, many thanks to my family, especially Rachael, Bernerd,

Aaron and Maddy, for continuing to humor this old man, and to my wife, Alice, whose support remains constant.